Barbara Maclou

May 95

D0364645

Dette Kim

Paper Craft

DAVID PORTEOUS
CHUDLEIGH · DEVON

CONTENTS

INTRODUCTION

Papercraft is one of the most popular of all crafts, and it is one that can be enjoyed by young and old alike. This book contains some of my favourite models, which are not only fun to make but are also fun to play with.

Next to the title of each project is a number in square brackets to indicate the page on which the figures are illustrated. All the projects are illustrated in full colour so that you can see what the finished articles look like, but you can use whatever colours you wish. Artists' suppliers and craft shops sell such wide ranges of card in different colours, finishes and weights that you are certain to find some unusual colours that will make your projects individual and personal to you.

Every project is accompanied by full-size templates, which you can transfer directly to the card or paper of your choice without having to worry about adjusting the size. If you prefer, of course, you can enlarge or reduce the templates on a photocopier or by the grid method to make the figures whatever size you like.

The first section describes the materials and equipment you will need and it also includes some hints about cutting and folding card and paper. It is a good idea to read these pages before you begin to work on one of the models.

Have fun!

Dette Kim

HOW TO FOLD

All the projects in this book are made from folded paper or card. For best results, you must make sure that all the folds are clean and sharp, and it is, therefore, a good idea to score the surface by running a darning needle or fine knitting needle along a ruler before you begin to fold. You must, though, be careful not to press so hard that the needle goes right through the paper or card – exert a steady, even pressure.

The fold lines on the templates are shown by two types of dotted line:

-------- indicates a mountain fold (fold up)

.... indicates a valley fold (fold down)

The illustrations on this page indicate the difference between the two types of fold. When you transfer the templates to your paper or card, draw in the fold lines with a soft pencil so that you can rub the marks out easily afterwards.

8

TEMPLATES

All the templates in the book are drawn to full size on a grid measuring 1 x 1cm (about $^3/_8$ x $^3/_8$in), which makes it easier to copy a template and, if necessary, to enlarge it.

If you want to enlarge a template so that it is twice the size, draw a grid with the same number of squares as the original, but make the squares 2 x 2cm (about $^3/_4$ x $^3/_4$in). Find a starting point on the original template and find the corresponding square in your new grid. Mark the points at which lines cross the squares, then join up the points so that you eventually draw the whole image, square by square.

If the template is going to be used at the original size, either copy it on to tracing paper or photocopy it. You can then transfer the outlines to your paper or card using carbon paper.

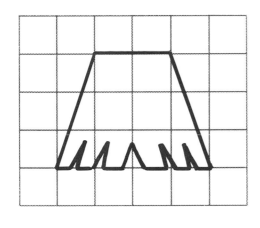

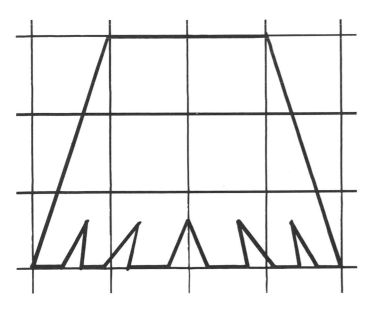

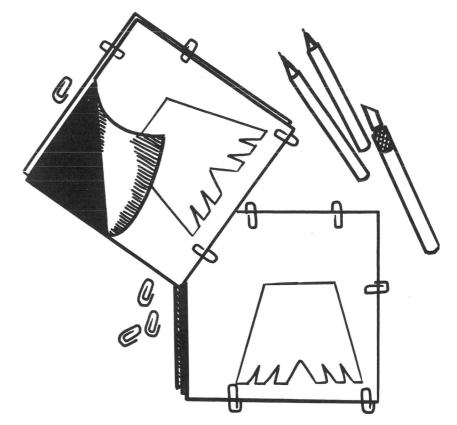

EQUIPMENT AND MATERIALS

To get the best results, you need to use the right equipment and materials. To make the projects in this book, you will need some or all of the following, so make sure you have them ready before you start.

Carbon paper Use carbon paper to transfer a drawing or template from one piece of paper or card to another. Never transfer a design directly from the book. Instead, draw the template on tracing paper or photocopy it, then place a sheet of carbon paper on the paper or card, place the tracing or copy over the carbon paper and go over the outline with a pencil.

Card All the models shown in this book have been made from card, which is available in lots of different weights and colours. Card that weighs 150–180gsm (56– 67lb) would be suitable for small, lightweight boxes, but when the instructions refer to thin card, you should use something that is rather more robust – 190–220gsm (70–82lb) would be suitable. If you make larger items you might need to use a card that weighs about 250gsm (94lb). Most stationers and shops that stock artists' materials will have a wide range of card and should be able to help you select an appropriate weight for your particular needs.

Compasses Use a pair of compasses when you want to draw circles or smooth curves.

Craft knife A craft knife is often easier to use than a pair of scissors. The best and cheapest kinds are those in which the blade is located within the body of the knife and sections are snapped off as they wear down. You could also use a scalpel, but remember that both tools can be dangerous and must always be used with care.

Cutting mat If you use a craft knife to cut around a template, it is a good idea to work on a special, non-slip mat. These mats are available from shops specializing in artists' materials and will protect your work surface. Alternatively, use a large piece of thick cardboard.

Darning needle Use a darning needle or blunt-ended tapestry needle to score fold lines (see page 8).

Eraser Remember to rub out fold lines and any guidelines you draw in before finishing off the projects and before applying paint.

Felt-tipped pens Keep a good selection of colours to draw eyes and other facial features and to decorate your projects.

Glue gun This is a convenient way of applying glue. The glue is melted inside the gun, and it is, therefore, warm when it comes out, although it does cool down as it dries. Take care that you don't burn yourself on the melted glue.

Glue stick Glue sticks are easier to use and are probably the safest kind of adhesive for children to use.

Hole punch Eye shapes can often be simply cut out with a hole punch. The plier kind are easiest to use, but you can also use a normal hole punch, although positioning the holes may be a little more difficult.

Paint Water-based paints have been used to decorate some of the projects.

Paper Many of the smaller items in this book have been made from Tivoli paper, which is very light – about 80gsm (35lb). You can buy this in stationery and craft shops, and it is available in many colours.

Paper clips Keep some paper clips handy to hold pieces of paper together while the glue dries. You can also use small bulldog clips.

Pencil Use a soft pencil for drawing on paper or card so that you can rub out the lines easily.

Photocopier If you have access to one, a photocopier is the simplest way to transfer a template to paper or card. It is also an easy way of enlarging or reducing a template, which can then be transferred to paper or card by using carbon paper.

Pinking shears These are perfect for creating neat zigzag edges.

Ruler You will need a ruler for measuring and marking the card. If you also use it for cutting against, make sure that you use a steel rule or one with a metal edge.

Scissors Ideally, keep one large pair and one small pair of scissors just for cutting paper and card.

Stapler You can often use staples instead of glue to hold together two pieces of paper, but remember to use staples only where they cannot be seen.

Tweezers A pair of tweezers can be useful for pressing small folds into place.

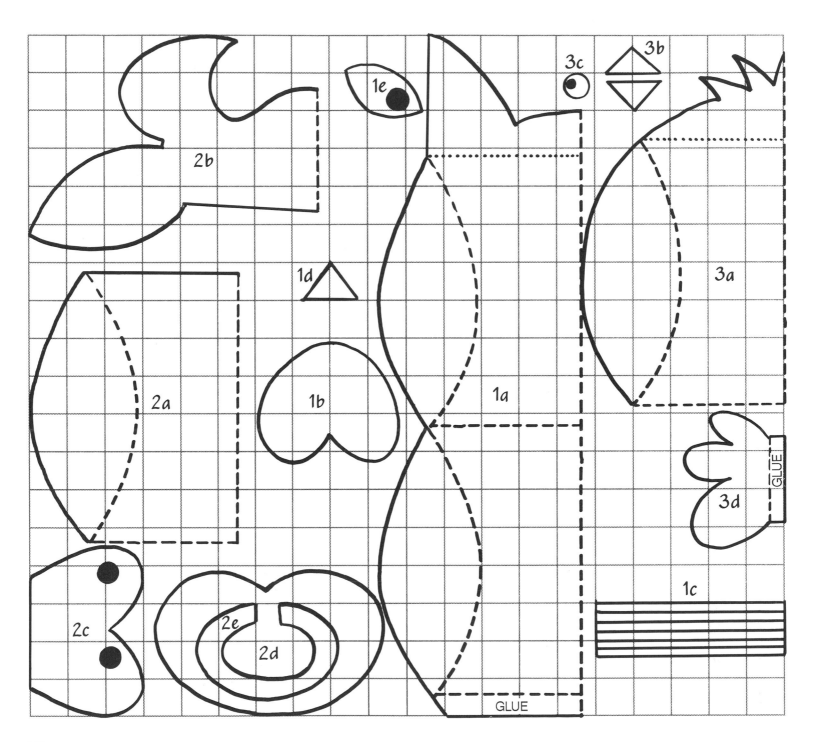

FLAT BOXES [15]

These flat boxes are all made from the same basic design. The templates are on pages 12 and 14, and they are identified as follows:

Cat 1a = body (cut out double); 1b = part of nose; 1c = whiskers; 1d = part of nose; 1e = eye (cut two).
Bull 2a = body (quarter template shown); 2b = horn and ear (cut out double); 2c = eyes; 2d = nose; 2e = ring.
Chicken 3a = body (quarter template shown); 3b = beak; 3c = eye (cut two); 3d = wing (cut two).
Tiger 4a = body (cut out double); 4b = eyes; 4c = part of nose; 4d = whiskers; 4e = part of nose.
Elephant 5a = body (quarter template shown); 5b = tusks; 5c = trunk.
Rabbit 6a = body (quarter template shown); 6b = teeth; 4c = part of nose; 4e = part of nose.

The basic shape of the box is the same for all the animals, with only the ears, horns and so on varying. To make the cat or tiger box, simply double the template. Draw a faint pencil line down the centre of a piece of card and lay the straight edge of the template against it. Draw around the template, turn it over, keeping the centre on the line, and draw around it again to create a mirror image of the first side.

The other body templates represent a quarter of the shape. Draw around the template, turn it over, keeping the centre carefully against the line you have already drawn, and draw around the shape again. The lower parts of the bull, chicken, elephant and rabbit are the same as the lower part of the cat or the tiger.

Score along the curved dotted lines. Fold in the tab for glue and glue the back to the top of the front. When the glue is dry, you can open and close the box by folding the curved sides in and out.

Attach the features the different animals as shown in the colour illustration on page 15. Fold back the elephant's ears and glue them to the back of the box. Use a black felt-tipped pen to draw on the tiger's stripes.

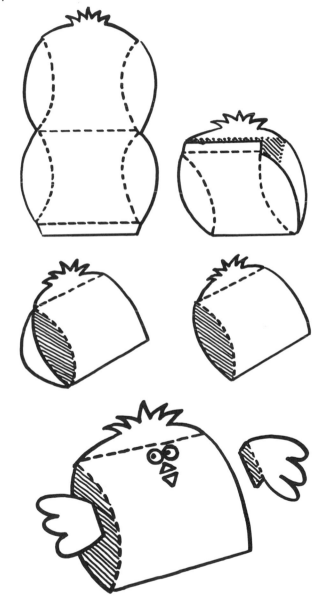

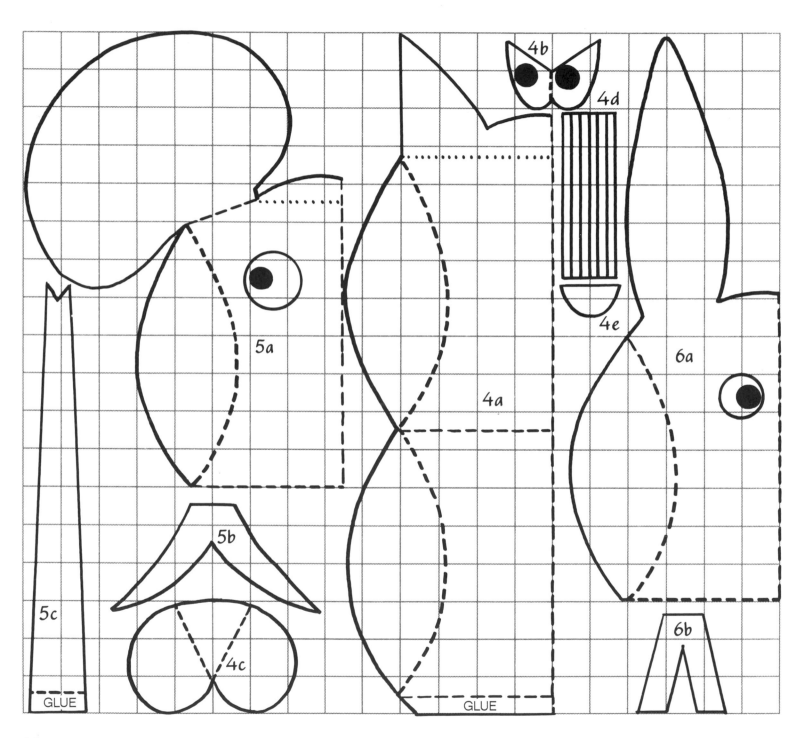

14

Flat boxes (see page 13).

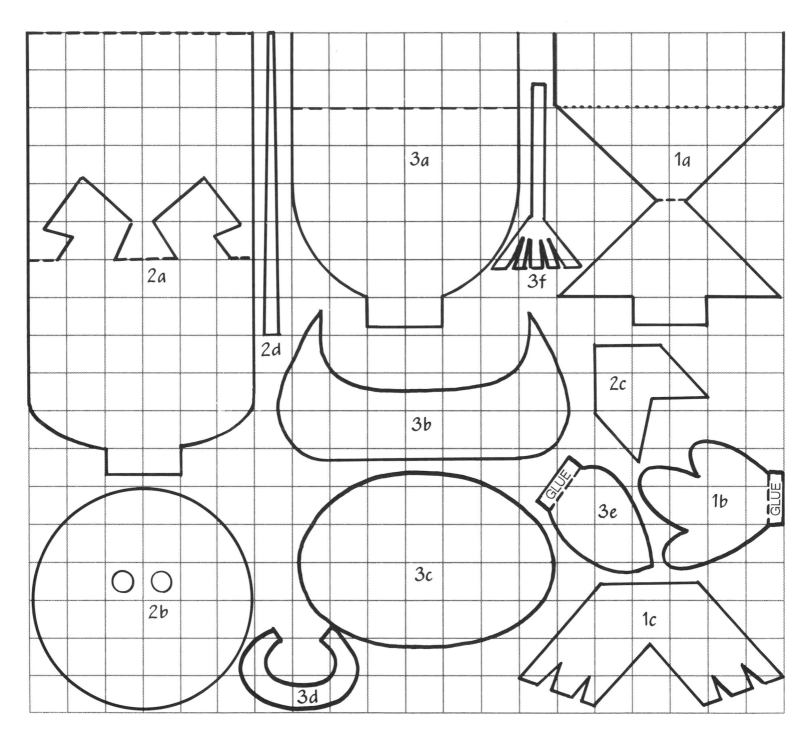

SQUARE BOXES [19]

These boxes are made in the same way as the flat boxes on page 13. The templates are on pages 16 and 18, and they are identified as follows:

Bird 1a = front; 1b = wing and tail (cut three); 1c = feet.

Pig 2a = front, top and ears; 2b = snout; 2c = foot (cut two); 2d = tail.

Bull 3a = front; 3b = horns; 3c = nose; 3d = ring; 3e = ear (cut two); 3f = tail.

Elephant 4a = front and top (extend the trunk to 7cm/ 2¾in); 4b = tusks; 4c = foot and toe nails (cut two of each); 4d = ear (cut two); 4e = tail.

Frog 5a = front, top and eyelids; 5b = upper mouth; 5c = eyes; 5d = front feet (cut two); 5e = back legs (cut two).

Use the outline on this page to draw and cut out the basic box shape. All the sides should measure 6 x 6cm (about 2½ x 2½in), except for the frog, which should be 5cm (2in) high or it will look out of proportion.

The fronts of the boxes – on pages 16 and 18 – should be added as shown in the colour illustration on page 19 (the bull is illustrated on the front cover). Glue the boxes together and seal them by pushing down the little flap into the notch in the front panel. You can work out the position and width of the notch by noting where the flap is when the box is closed.

The bird's beak should be slightly open. The elephant has a trunk in place of a flap; instead of cutting one notch, cut two notches and run the trunk through at the front.

Use the colour illustration as a guide for attaching the eyes, ears and so on. We added a small section of thick card under the pig's snout and the bull's nose so that the faces look more three-dimensional. Glue the frog's eyes along the inside top edge of the front of the box so that they are visible through the openings in the front section.

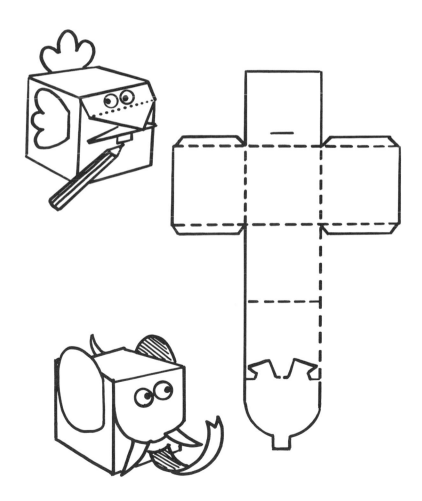

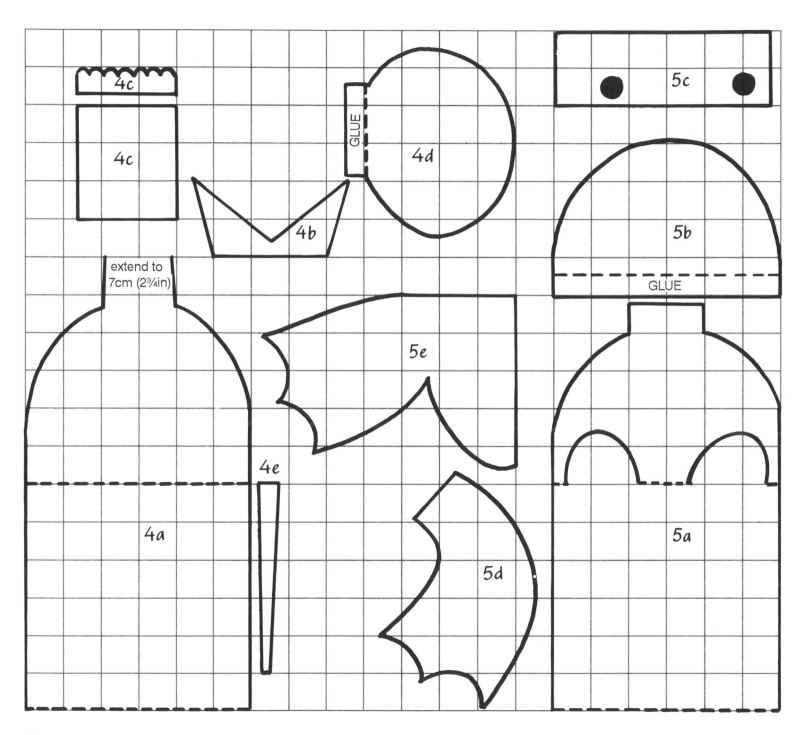

4c

4c

4d

GLUE

5c

4b

5b

GLUE

extend to
7cm (2¾in)

5e

4e

4a

5d

5a

18

Square boxes (see page 17).

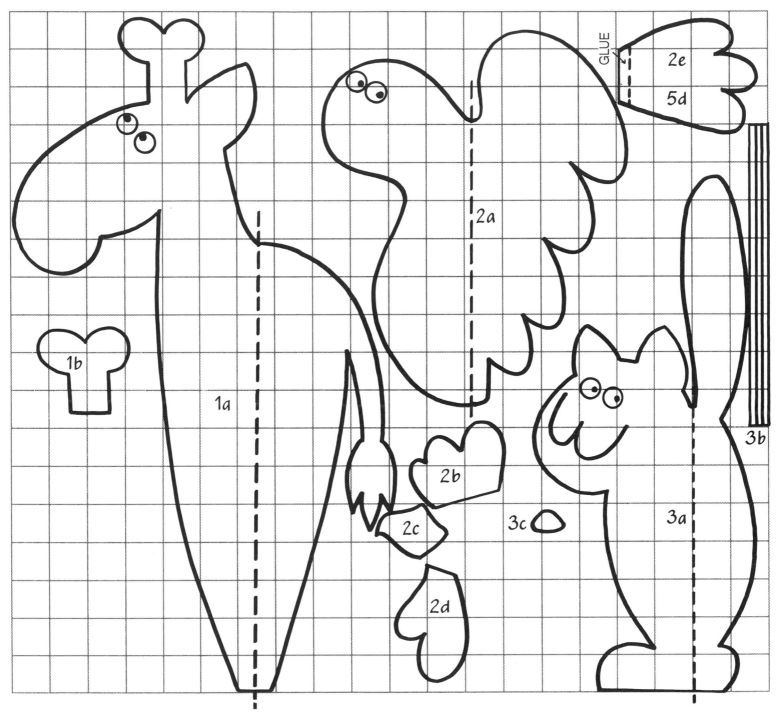

OPEN BOXES [23]

These boxes can be used to hold pencils or brushes or perhaps sweets for a children's party. The templates are on pages 20 and 22, and they are identified as follows:

Giraffe 1a = body; 1b = horns.
Cockerel 2a = body; 2b = cock's comb; 2c = beak; 2d = wattle; 2e = wing (cut two).
Cat 3a = body; 3b = whiskers; 3c = nose.
Rabbit 4a = body; 4b = eye (cut two); 4c = nose; 4d = teeth.
Duck 5a = body; 5b = beak; 5c = bow tie; 5d = wing (cut two, see page 20).
Elephant 6a = body; 6b = ear (cut two); 6c = tusk (cut two).
Reindeer 7a = body.

The centre sections of the templates have not been included to save space, but the illustrations below show how they should be drawn. You can make the centre section as large as you wish, and you can easily adjust the height of the template to keep the box in proportion by using the grid method. Cut out a back section, with two 5mm (¼in) flaps that can be glued to the head and tail ends. Remember that the back section must be exactly the same size as the front section. The illustrations on this page show how the back section is folded and glued to create the box shape.

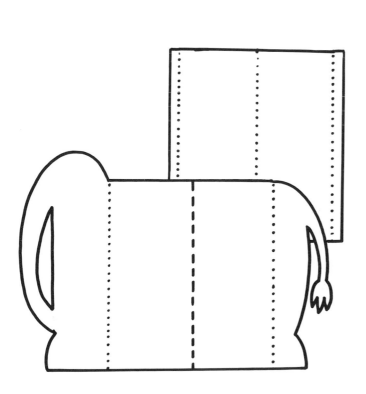

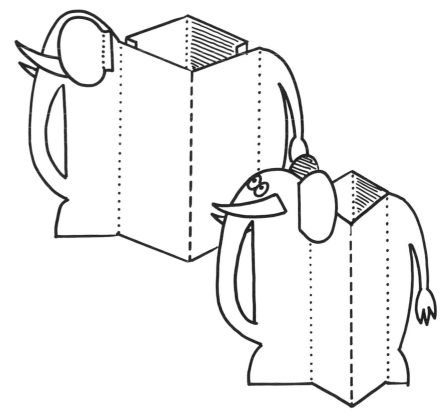

21

GLUE

6b

6c

7a

4c

5c

5b

6a

4a

5a

4b

4d

Open boxes (see page 21).

23

PIRATES [27]

The different parts of the pirates can be combined or varied in whatever ways you wish. They are made in the same way as the clowns on page 29. The templates are on pages 24 and 26, and they are identified as follows:

All pirates 1a = front of head; 1b = back of head; 2 = short-sleeved jacket (cut out double); 3 = arm or sleeve (cut two); 4a = leg (cut one or two); 4b = wooden leg (optional).
First pirate 5b = moustache; 5c = kerchief; 5d = belt; 5e = buckle; 5g = sword; 5h = pistol.
Second pirate 5a = beard; 5c = kerchief; 5d = belt; 5e = buckle; 5g = sword; 6i = dagger.
Pirate captain 6a = hat; 6b = hat decoration; 6c = eye patch; 6d = moustache; 6e = epaulettes (cut two); 6f = cuffs (cut two); 6g = hook; 6h = hand; 6j = shoulder strap; 6k = sabre; 6l = hair; 5f = dagger.

Make the heads in the same way as the heads of the clowns (see page 29). Fold the nose up slightly and glue the moustache or moustache and beard under the nose. Fold the arms or sleeves and glue them together. To make the curved lines fold properly, score along the lines with a darning needle or a fine knitting needle. If you are making the captain, do not cut out the hands when you cut around the sleeve template (number 3). Push the neck through the top of the slot in the centre top of the jacket, which should be glued together around the arms. The arms can point either upwards or downwards, as shown in the colour illustration on page 27.

Fold the captain's hat in the same way you folded the arms and glue the hat together at the tips to keep it in shape. Use two small strips of card to glue the hat on to the head (see colour illustration), and then glue on all the different accessories as you wish.

Attach the legs by pushing them into the slots in the bottom edges of the jacket.

Pirates (see page 25).

CLOWNS [31]

Festive clowns are always colourful and full of fun, and these bright figures are made in much the same way as the pirates on page 25. The templates are on pages 28 and 30, and they are identified as follows:

All clowns 1a = front of head; 1b = back of head; 2 = arm or sleeve (cut two).
Blue clown 3a = hair; 3b = hat; 3c = flower stalk; 3d = flower; 3e = eye (cut two); 3f = white mouth; 3g = red mouth; 3h = shirt (cut out double); 3i = bow tie; 3j = glove (cut four); 3k = boot (cut two).
Red and white clown 4a = hair; 4b = eye (cut two); 4c = white mouth; 4d = red mouth; 4e = shirt (cut out double); 4f = tie; 4g = collar; 4h = sleeve (cut two); 4i = glove (cut four); 4j = shoe (cut two).
White clown 5a = eye (cut two); 5b = hat; 5c = shirt (cut out double); 5d = collar; 5e = hands (cut two); 5 = legs (cut two).

Only cut around the outline of the nose on the white clown. Push the top and bottom points of the front head section through the slots in the back head section. Glue the appropriate eyes, mouths and hair on to the heads as shown in the colour illustration on page 31. The round, red noses are small wooden beads. Use a red felt-tipped pen to draw on the eyebrows and mouth on the white clown's face and add a couple of stars in black.

Assemble the arms in the same way as the arms of the pirates (see page 25). Push the neck though the slot in the centre top of the shirt, which should be glued together around the arms. The arms can point either upwards or downwards. Attach the boots or legs by fitting the slots into the corresponding slots in the bottom edges of the shirt.

Glue on the accessories as you wish. We cut the striped shirt out of red card and stuck strips of white paper on to it, but you could use paints or felt-tipped pens.

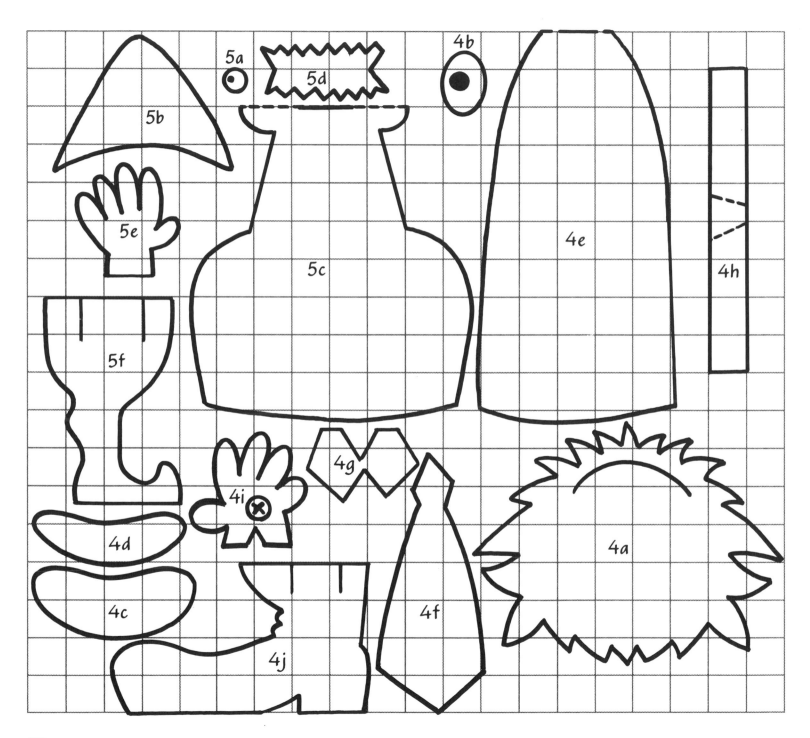

30

Clowns (see page 29).

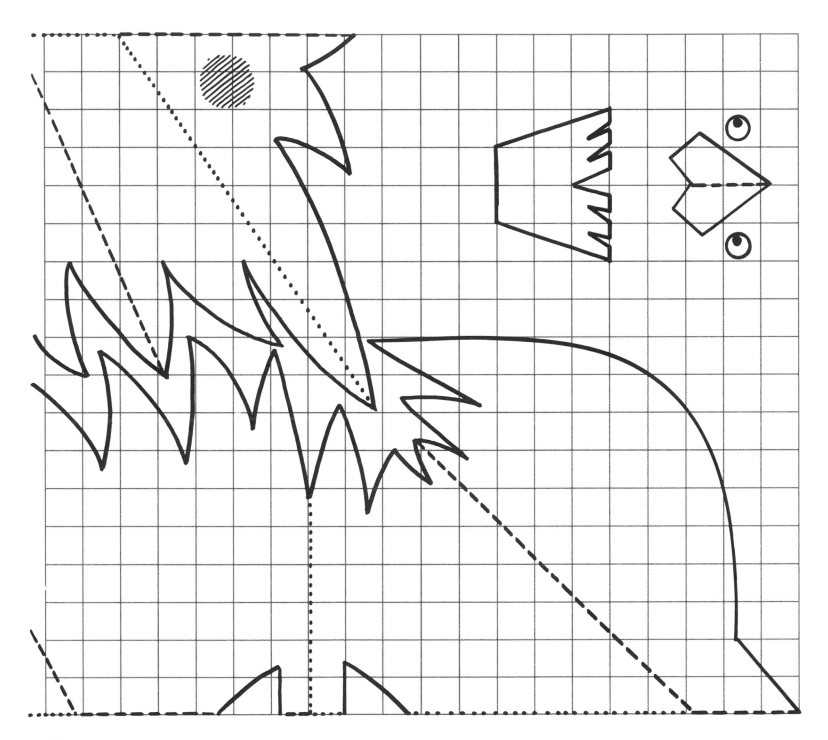

LYRE BIRD [35]

This bird is folded out of a single piece of card, with just the beak, eyes and feet being attached separately. Transfer the templates to a piece of card, placing them together as shown in the illustration below. Fold the card in two and place the template against the fold before cutting it out.

Fold the bird along the dotted lines and add a few spots of adhesive between the outer ends of the tail to hold the bird together (the shaded areas on the template show where you should add the glue).

Cut out two beaks and two eyes and glue them in place. Attach the feet underneath the body.

PEACOCK [35]

The peacock is made from a single sheet of card, with only the crest, feet, eyes and beak being cut out separately. Fold the card and lay the centre line of the template against the fold. Score along the lines, making sure you differentiate between the mountain and valley folds, so that you can fold the tail easily.

Fold the head upwards and outwards as shown in the illustrations below. Glue the inside of the triangular opening together; the shaded area on the template indicates where to apply the adhesive.

Glue the feet underneath the body and then glue the beak and eyes onto the head. Cut some fine strips to form a crest and glue it to the top of the head. Finally, if you wish, decorate the edge of the tail as shown in the illustration.

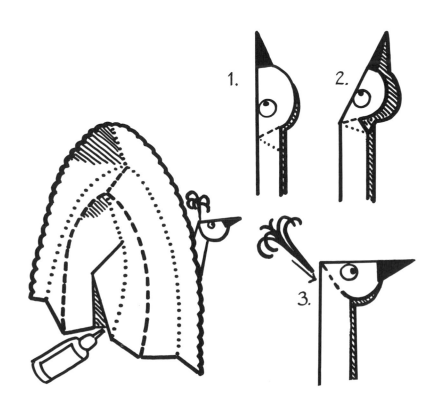

Lyre bird (see page 33); peacock (see page 34).

1c

1b

1e

1h

1a

1g

1f

1d

36

TABLE DECORATIONS [39]

You could use some table decorations like these for a child's birthday party. The templates are on pages 36 and 38, and they are identified as follows:

Clowns 1a = body (cut out double); 1b = eye (cut two); 1c = nose and mouth; 1d = hair; 1e = bowler hat; 1f = pointed hat; 1g = bow tie; 1h = tie.
Place cards 2a = name card; 2b = glove; 2c = hat.
Napkin holder 3a = glove.

Glue the clown's hat on its head and glue on the eyes. Attach the nose and mouth by means of the point at the top of nose – push it up through the slot in the head and fold it down at the back. Glue the hair on the back of the head to cover up the point.

Glue on a tie or a bow tie. If you wish, cut out white gloves to cover the hands and glue them on. Glue the arms and legs together at the front of the body so that they will go around a glass.

Glue the small glove to one of the place cards so that it looks as if the arm is sticking out when the card is closed. Glue the hat to the other card at the upper folded edge. Use the large glove to hold a napkin.

2a

2c

2b

3a

Table decorations (see page 37).

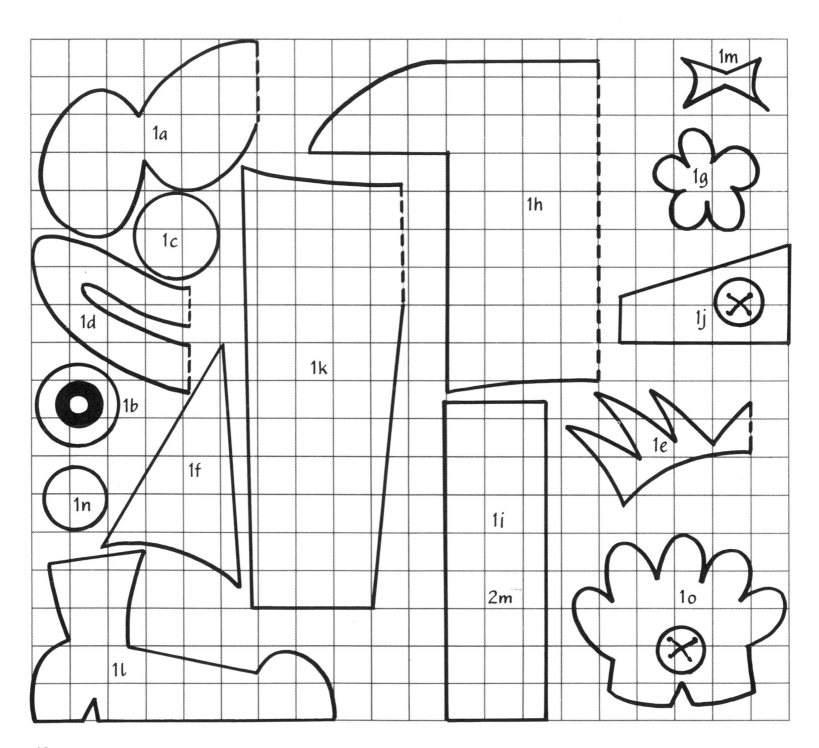

1a
1c
1d
1b
1n
1f
1l
1k
1h
1i
2m
1m
1g
1j
1e
1o

CLOWNS AND RING MASTER [43]

The ring master and clowns are made in the same way. Each figure has a thread through the top so that it can be hung up to turn around like a mobile. The faces are double because they are seen from both sides. The templates are on pages 40 and 42, and they are identified as follows:

Clowns 1a = upper part of head (cut two, cutting out double); 1b = eye (cut four); 1c = nose (cut two); 1d = mouth (cut two, cutting out double); 1e = hair (cut out double); 1f = pointed hat (cut two); 1g = flower on top of hat (cut two); 1h = shirt (cut out double); 1i = arm (cut two); 1j = cuff with buttons (cut four); 1k = trousers (cut out double); 1l = boot (cut two); 1m = bow for boot (cut two); 1n = button for stripy clown (cut six); 1o = glove (cut two).

Ring master 2a = jacket (cut out double); 2b = head (cut two); 2c = eye (cut four); 2d = moustache (cut two, cutting out double); 2e = hair (cut two); 2f = hat (cut two, cutting out double); 2g = bow tie (cut two); 2h = shirt front (cut two); 2i = jacket revers (cut four); 2j = epaulettes (cut four); 2k = pocket (cut four); 2l = braid for jacket (cut six); 2m = arm (cut two, see page 40); 2n = cuff (cut four); 2o = glove (cut two); 2p trousers (cut out double); 2q = boot (cut two).

Assemble the figures as shown in the colour illustration on page 43.

To make the clowns, glue a mouth, a nose and two eyes to a head section, then glue the two head sections together around the hair. One of the clowns has no trousers but a long shirt and the boots are simply attached to the bottom edge of the shirt.

The ring master is made in the same way. Glue the shirt front to the jacket, then attach the revers, then glue on the bow tie.

2c 2d 2f 2o 2b 2e 2k 2l 2h 2a 2j 2p 2q 2g 2i 2n

42

Clowns and ring master (see page 41).

FISH [47]

The fish on this page and the chicken and bird on the next pages are all made from a single, long strip of card.

Copy the templates, placing them so that they are in a single piece as shown below. Score and fold the card along the dotted lines and glue the strip together to form a ring. Fold the two tail fins inwards and glue them in place, then fold the ends out again. The shaded areas on the template show you where to apply the adhesive.

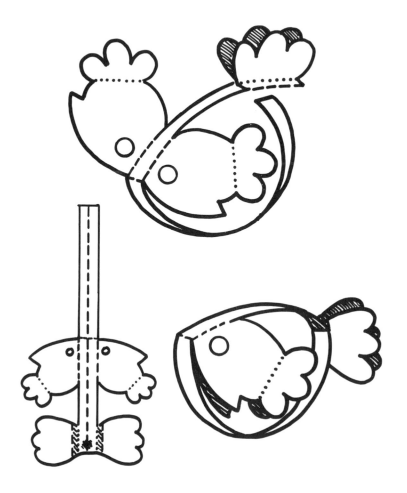

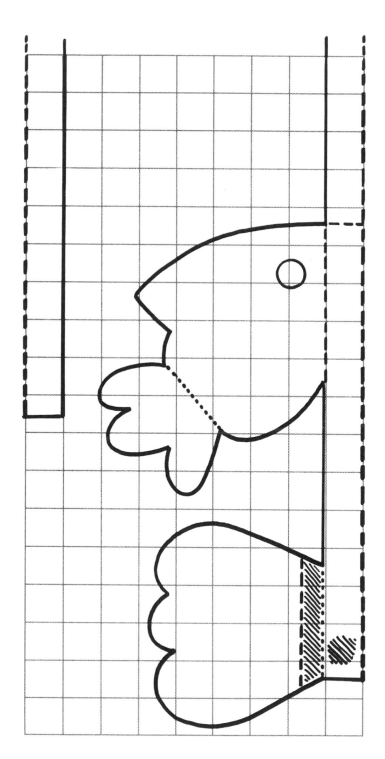

44

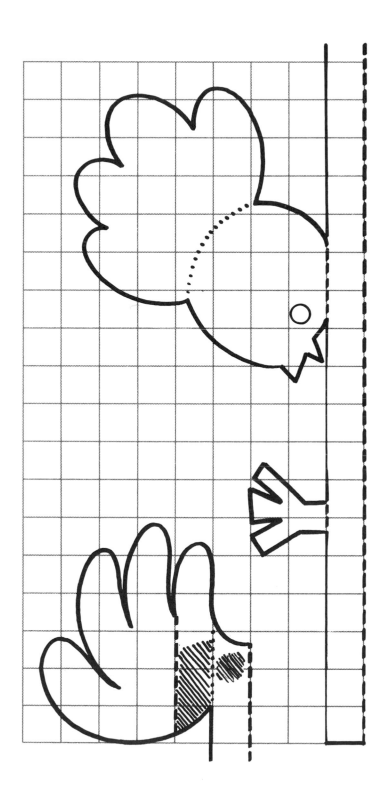

CHICKEN [47]

Make the chicken in the same way as the fish.

Copy the templates, arranging them as a single piece as shown below. Score and fold the card, and glue the strip together to form a ring. Fold the tail feathers inwards and glue them in place, then bend the ends out again. The shaded areas on the template show you where to apply the adhesive.

45

BIRD [47]

Make the bird in the same way as the fish and the chicken.

Copy the three templates and arrange them as a single piece as shown below. Start with the head, which is shaped like a little ring, then shape the body and fold the eyes down over the head. Fold along the dotted lines to form the beak. Glue the tail to the back of the body. The shaded areas on the template show you where to apply the glue.

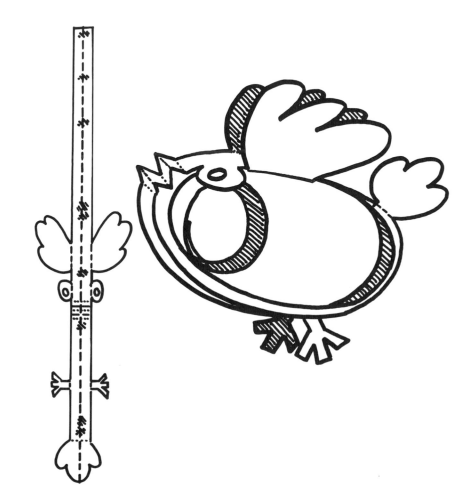

Fish (see page 44); chickens (see page 45); birds (see page 46).

48

CIRCUS ACTS [51]

These small figures are suitable for the circus ring described on page 50, and the illustration on page 51 shows how the figures should be assembled. The templates are on page 48, and they are identified as follows:

Horse 1a = body; 1b = head and neck; 1c = mane (cut out double); 1d = saddle; 1e = decoration; 1f = bow; 1g = tail.

Clowns 2a = body; 2b = head; 2c = pointed hat; 2d = bowler hat; 2e = ball; 2f = chair; 2g = mouth; 2h = nose, eyes and buttons; 2j = hair; 2l = tie; 2m = glove (cut two); 2n = feet.

Acrobat 3a = body; 3b = head; 3c = hat; 3d = hat decoration; 3e = moustache; 3f = waistcoat; 3g = hand (cut two); 3h feet.

Ring master 4a = body; 4b = head; 4c = hat; 4d = moustache; 4e = eyes and buttons; 4f = epaulettes (cut two); 4g = glove (cut two); 4h = trousers; 4i = whip.

Glue the neck of the horse around the body, with the mane between the fold in the back of the neck. Then glue the tail, saddle and decoration to the horse.

Assemble the figures. Attach the clown's feet by pushing them up into the slots in the bottom of the body. Glue the acrobat's feet between the front and back of the body as shown.

Bend the ring master's feet forwards and outwards, gluing the longer feet on the outside so that the figure will stand upright.

CIRCUS RING [51]

This ring is suitable for the artistes described on pages 48–9. The templates for the circus ring are on pages 52–3, and the illustration below shows how the templates should be arranged on the card. Use a pair of compasses to draw the curved section – it should be 20cm (8in) in diameter. Fold down the flaps in the opening and glue them to the back section. Glue the flap at the bottom of the back section under the curved part of the ring (see the illustration below right).

Use the template (top right) to cut out two curtains, and cut out two ties, attaching them as shown. Glue the top of the curtains around a thin piece of wire so that they can hang up inside the opening.

Cut out the letters of the word "circus" in different coloured paper and glue them above the opening. Use the illustration for ideas on how to decorate the circus ring.

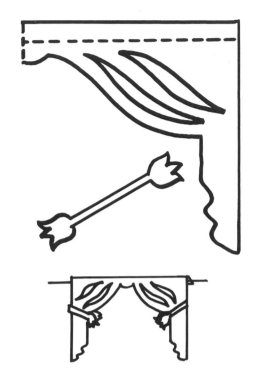

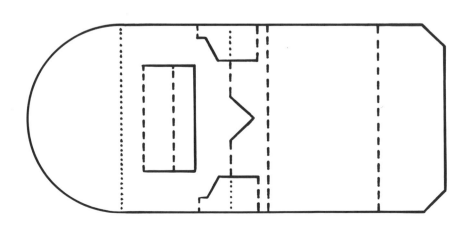

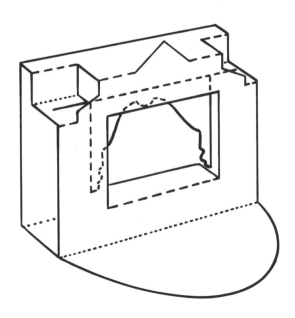

Circus acts (see page 49); circus ring (see page 50).

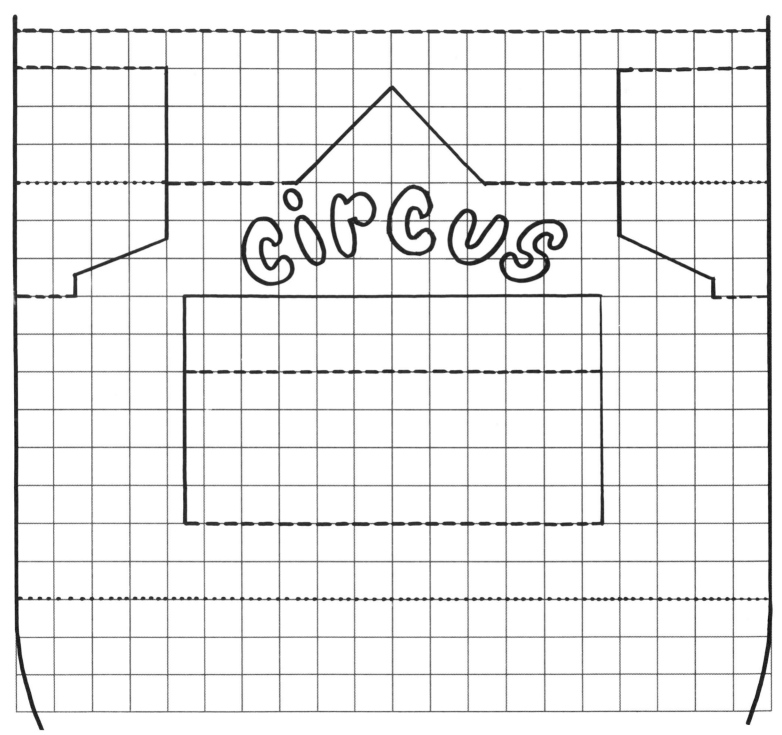

52

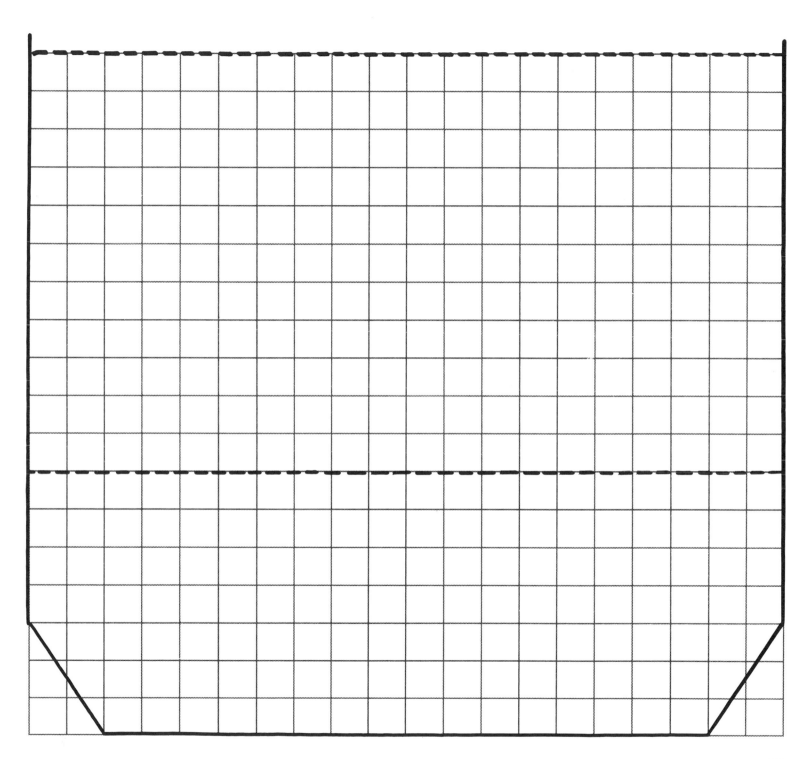

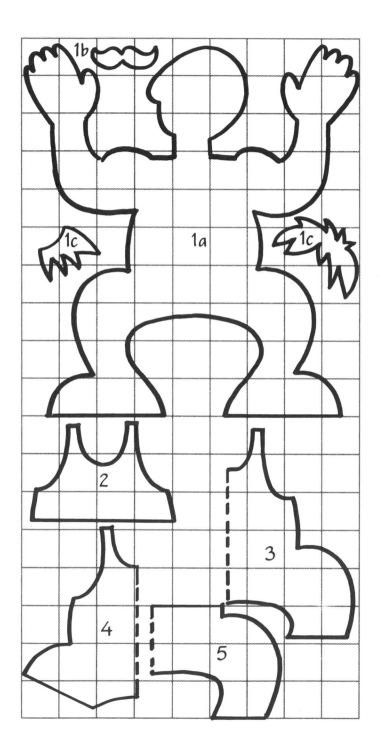

STRONG MEN [55]

The idea is to arrange the strong men so that they are in the most amazing acrobatic positions. You could, for example, arrange them in a pyramid as if they were about to catch another member of the team. The templates are on the left, and they are identified as follows:

1a = body; 1b = moustache; 1c = hair; 2 = singlet; 3 = long-legged costume (cut out double); 4 = short-legged costume (cut out double); 5 = trousers (cut out double).

Dress the acrobats as shown in the colour illustration on page 55. This will also give you some idea of how to arrange them. To give extra stability, glue the figures together when you arrange them. As the illustration below shows, you can also make the figures do handstands.

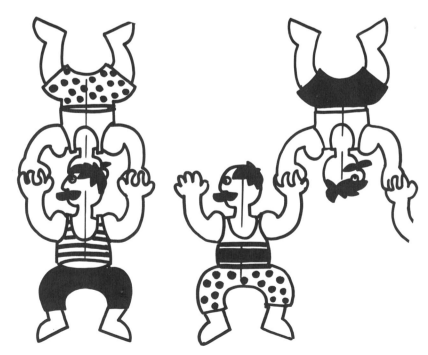

Strong men (see page 54).

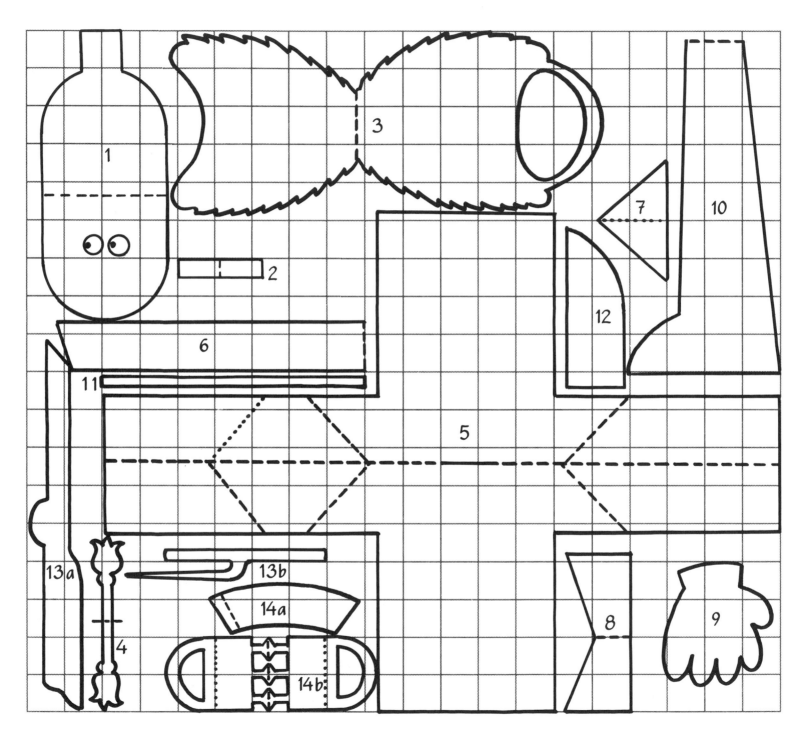

56

GUARDSMEN [59]

These dashing red guardsmen march along in time to music. The templates are on page 56, and they are identified as follows:

1 = head; 2 = shirt collar; 3 = bearskin; 4 = tassels; 5 = jacket; 6 = cross-piece (cut two, cutting out double); 7 = epaulette (cut two); 8 = cuff (cut two); 9 = glove (cut two); 10 = leg (cut out double); 11 = braid for trousers (cut two); 12 = shoe (cut two); 13a = rifle butt; 13b = barrel and bayonet of rifle; 14a = horn of trumpet; 14b = handle and valves of trumpet.

Fold the head along the dotted line so that the neck is at the back. Glue the shirt collar around the neck. Fold the hat together and glue it around the head. Glue on the tassel between the head and strap. Push the neck down into the slot in the top of the jacket. Fold the sleeves down along the dotted lines. Glue on the epaulettes between the shoulders, glue on the gloves, then cover the join by gluing on the cuffs. Glue the cross-pieces to the front and back of the jacket. Glue the braid and shoes to the trousers, and fold and glue these between the two sections of the jacket.

Bend the arms into the shape you want, depending on what the guardsman will be carrying – look at the illustration on page 59 to see how the arms should be bent.

Make the trumpet as shown in the illustration. Roll a thin tube out of a piece of very lightweight paper measuring 4 x 2.5cm (1½ x 1in). Around this tube, roll another from a piece of paper measuring 3.5 x 3cm (1¼ x 1 ⅛in). Glue the handle with valves around the tubes as shown. Finally, glue the horn to the end of the trumpet.

Make a drum from a piece of card measuring about 12 x 2.5cm (4¾ x 1in) and glue it to two circles, each 3.5cm (1¼in) in diameter. The drumsticks are small rolls of paper, as are the flute and the flagstaff. The straps for the drum and flagstaff are thin strips with tassels at the ends, and the flautist's music is held by a small piece of wire glued to the shoulder.

SENTRY BOX [59]

The sentry box is in proportion to the soldiers on page 57. Transfer the template shown left to card, increasing the number of sides to eight and lengthening the sides so that they are 19cm (7½in) high. Glue the sides together.

The roof is held together with a little rosette as shown in the illustration. Glue strips of white paper around the top and bottom of the box to finish it off.

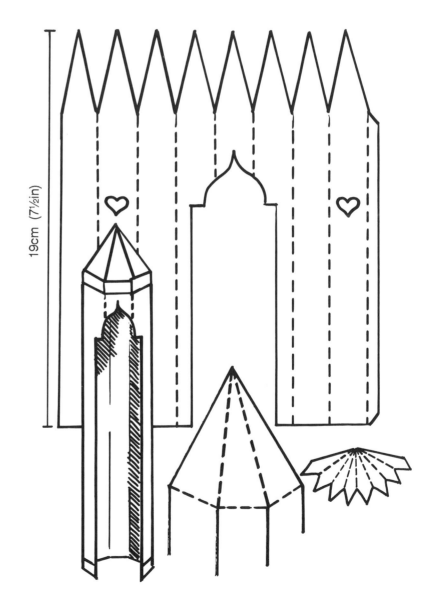

Guardsmen (see page 57); sentry box (see page 58).

BIRDS AND FLOWERS [63]

The birds shown in the templates on page 60 and the flowers in the template on page 62 are easy to keep in position because they have pegs on the back. They would be ideal decorations for a summer party. The templates are identified as follows:

Birds 1a = body of small bird; 1b = wings and tail of both birds; 1c = feet of small bird; 1d = eyes of small bird; 1e = beak of small bird; 1f = crest of small bird; 2a = body of large bird; 2b = wings and tail of large bird (cut three); 2c = feet of large bird; 2d = eyes of large bird; 2e = beak of large bird; 2f = crest of large bird.

Flowers 3a = daisy (cut out double); 3b = centre of daisy; 4a = blue flower (cut out double); 4b = centre of blue flower; 5a = poppy (cut out double); 5b = centre of poppy; 6a = tulip (cut out double).

Assemble the bird as shown in the illustration on this page, using the colour illustration on page 63 as a guide. Glue a small square of corrugated card between the body and the wing to create a three-dimensional effect.

Cut out and assemble the flowers as shown in the colour illustration on page 63, using a small piece of corrugated card to separate the two sizes of petals. Cut stamens and leaves for the tulip and attach them as illustrated.

Finally, glue a wooden clothes peg to the back of each flower and to the back of each bird.

Flowers and birds (see page 61).

FEEDING TIME [67]

The animals made here appear to bend forwards to eat the food placed in front of them. The templates are on pages 64 and 66, and they are identified as follows:

Chicken 1a = body (cut two); 1b = wing (cut two); 1c = foot (cut two); 1d = beak; 1e = food (cut 15–20).
Bee 2a = body (cut two); 2b = head; 2c = wings (cut two); 2d = antennae; 2e = sting; 2f = small flower and leaf; 2g = large flower and leaf; 2h = small leaf (cut two).
Duck 3a = body (cut two); 3b = wing (cut two); 3c = feet (cut out double); 3d beak (cut two); 3e = pond with grass.
Dog 4a = body (cut two); 4b = tail; 4c = bone (cut three).
Cat 5a = body (cut two); 5b = whiskers; 5c = nose; 5d =fish.
Butterfly 6a = wings (cut two, one of each size); 6b = spots on wings (cut four); 6c = body; 6d = head and antennae; 6e = base; 6f = leaf; 6g eyes.

When you have assembled the individual animals as described below, glue each one to a piece of oblong card, measuring 30 x 8cm (12 x 3¼in), and fold it as shown in the illustration. If you push the ends of the card inwards, the animal will seem to bend down to its food.

Glue the body of the chicken together and press the legs slightly outwards at the bottom so that you can glue them to the card between the feet. Fold the beak together and glue it around the head. Glue the wings on either side of the body.

Glue the two bee bodies together with the sting and antennae between them. Glue the head, with the eyes in place, to the front of the body and glue on the wings.

Draw on the black stripes with a felt-tipped pen. Bend the two small flaps at the bottom of the body slightly outwards and glue them to the card, covering them with small leaves.

Glue the duck's body together with the legs between. Glue the beak and the wings to either side of the body, then glue the feet to the card.

Glue the dog together so that the feet and ears bend outwards and so that the forelegs are slightly apart.

Glue the cat so that its legs bend outwards. Glue on the whiskers with the nose over them. Glue the feet to the card.

Glue the spots on the butterfly's wings and glue the two pairs of wings together, with the body on top. Bend the head upwards. Glue the base of the butterfly as shown in the illustration.

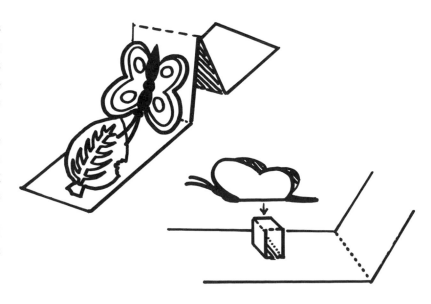

Feeding time (see page 65).

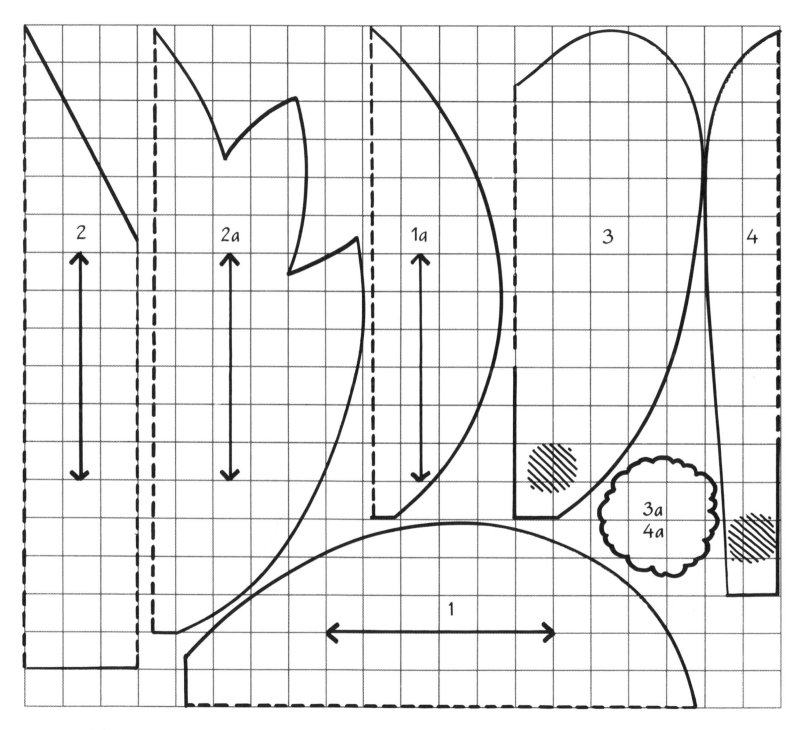

FLOWERS [71]

These colourful flowers are made from crepe paper and card. The great advantage of crepe paper is that you can pull it into shape so that it curves like real petals. The templates on page 68 are all half-templates, so you should place the central line along the fold in the paper. The arrows indicate the way in which the grain of the paper should lie. It's important to make sure that this is straight; if it is not, the petals will not curl properly.

Rose Use template 1 to make 10 petals. Carefully pull the petals into shape and gather them at the bottom around a strong piece of wire (florist's stubb wire is ideal), which will act as a stem. Hold the petals in place by winding a piece of thread or strong cotton tightly around them. Finish off by covering the stem and cotton with green florist's tape (which is available from most florist's shops). Beginning at the top, wind the tape around the bottoms of the petals, and then wind it evenly down the stem. About halfway down, add some leaves (made from template 1a).

Peony Copy template 2 so that it is double and draw it 10 times. Cut out the crepe paper and gently pull the ends of the petals outwards. Roll the flower up and make a stem from a length of wire. Finish off the stem as for the rose, adding leaves made from template 2a about halfway down the stem.

Poppy The poppy is made from card cut from template 3. You will need five petals altogether, which can be made to look more natural if you glue the bottom corners over each other, applying the adhesive as indicated on the template. Glue the centre, template 3a, in position, and make a stem, covered in green florist's tape, and glue it to the back of the flower.

Daisy The daisy is also made from card, and you will need 10 petals cut from template 4. Glue the bottom corners together with a spot of glue as indicated on the template before gluing the centre, template 4a, in place. You can make a stem in the same way as for the poppy.

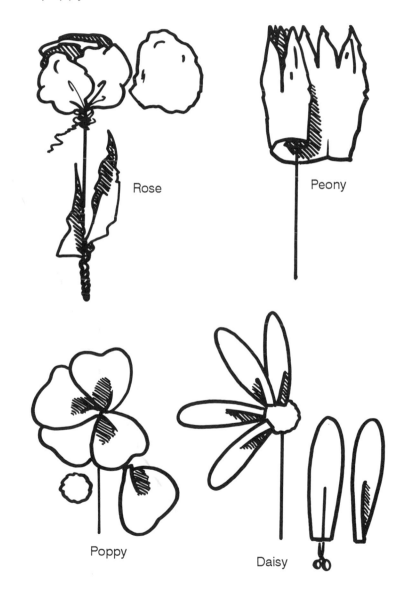

Rose

Peony

Poppy

Daisy

69

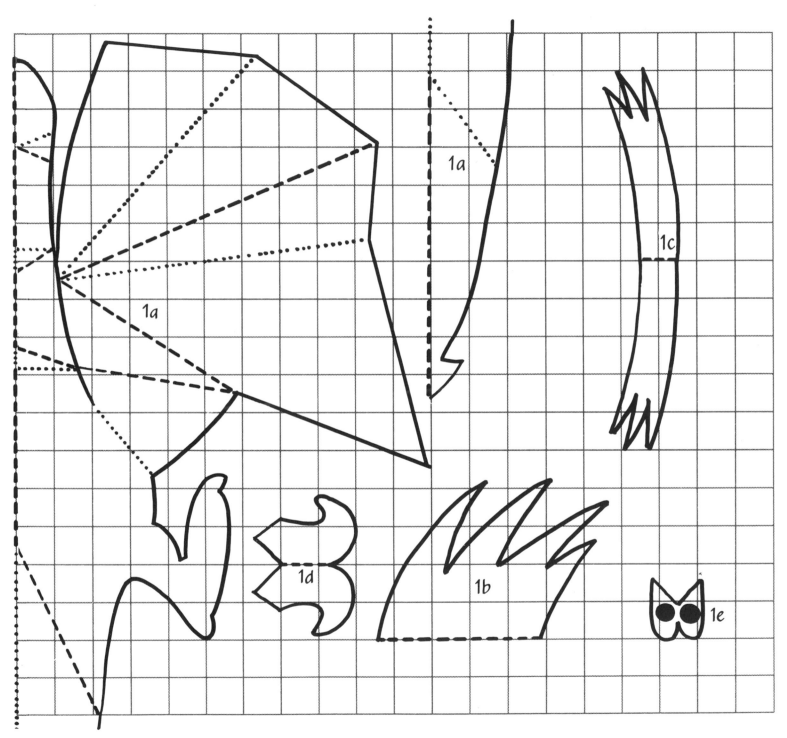

1a

1a

1c

1d

1b

1e

Flowers (see page 69).

PTERODACTYL AND DRAGON [75]

No one knows what colour prehistoric animals were, so you can make these creatures whatever colours you wish. We chose red with yellow spots for the pterodactyl, as you can see in the colour illustration on page 75. The templates for these two animals are on pages 70 and 73, and they are identified as follows:

Pterodactyl 1a = body (cut out double); 1b = spines (cut out double); 1c = front legs; 1d = beak; 1e = eyes.
Dragon 2a = body (cut out double); 2b = spines (cut out double); 2c = armour-plating (cut two of each piece); 2d = teeth (cut two); 2e = eye; 2f = flames.

Remember to add the tail end of the pterodactyl's body when you draw the template. Fold the body along the dotted lines, and glue the front legs under the body,

just behind the neck. Push the spines into the slot in the centre of the back and separate the points slightly. Glue the beak and eyes to the head.

Draw the template for the dragon as shown below, remembering to add the front leg and head pieces. Fold the body along the dotted lines and push the spines into the slot in the back, separating the points. Glue together the top of the top of the head and the upper jaw, applying the adhesive where indicated on the template. Pull the points of the flame over the edge of a blade of a knife or pair of scissors to make them curl, and glue them into the mouth before gluing the teeth on either side of the lower jaw. Finally, glue on the eyes.

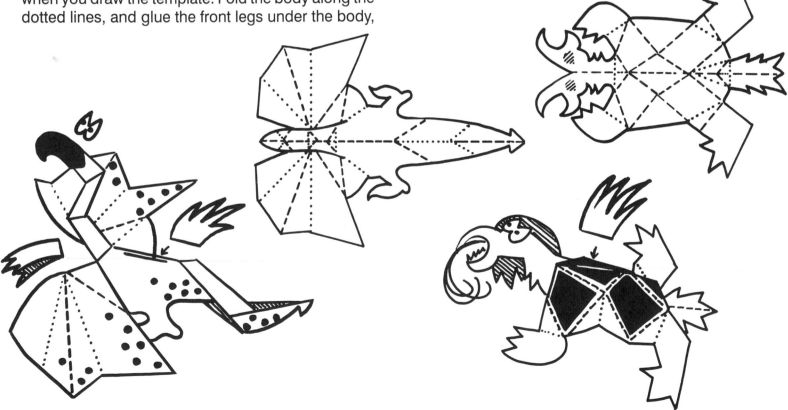

2f

2e

2b

2a

2c

2c

2d

2a

2c

2a

73

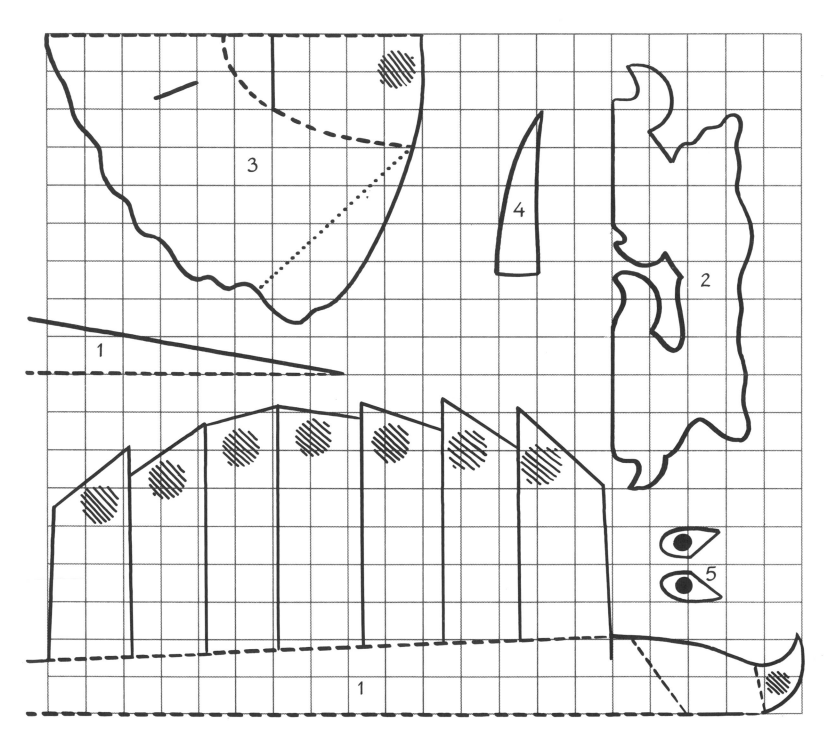

Pterodactyl and dragon (see page 72); stegosaurus (see page 76).

STEGOSAURUS [75]

This stegosaurus looks very fierce! The templates are on page 74, and they are identified as follows:

1 = body (cut out double); 2 = leg (cut four); 3 = armour-plating (cut out double); 4 = horns (cut three); 5 = eyes.

Transfer the template to a piece of card, remembering to add the tail piece as shown below. Fold the body along the dotted lines, laying the wide strips over each other and gluing them together, with the adhesive placed as indicated on the illustration below. If you wish, glue thin strips of paper down the sides of the body as shown in the colour illustration on page 75. Glue the legs, in pairs, along the bottom edge of the body.

  Fold the head into shape and glue together the two nose points, placing the adhesive as shown in the illustration. Shape the armour-plating for around the neck and push the head through the ruff so that it lies around the neck. Push the horns into the slots in the ruff and in the nose and glue in position. Glue on the eyes.

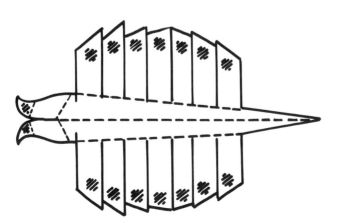

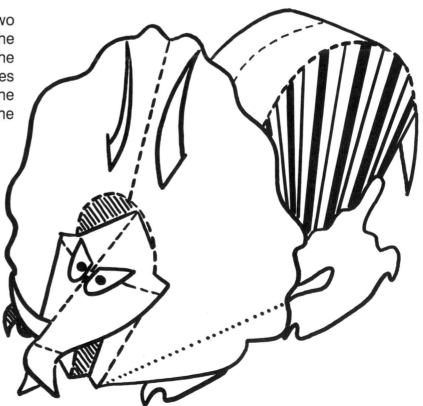

A CIP catalogue record for this book is available from the
British Library

ISBN 1 870586 22 0

Published by David Porteous
PO Box 5
Chudleigh
Newton Abbot
Devon TQ13 0YZ

Copyright © 1993 Forlaget Klematis
Danish edition copyright © 1993 Forlaget Klematis: Klip &
plynt for sjov
English edition copyright © 1994 David Porteous

All rights reserved.
No part of this publication may be reproduced, stored in a
retrieval system, or transmitted, in any form or by any means,
electronic, mechanical, photocopying, recording or otherwise,
without prior permission from the publisher.

Translated by Tim Bowler
Typeset by Blanc Verso
Printed and bound in Great Britain
by BPC Paulton Books Limited

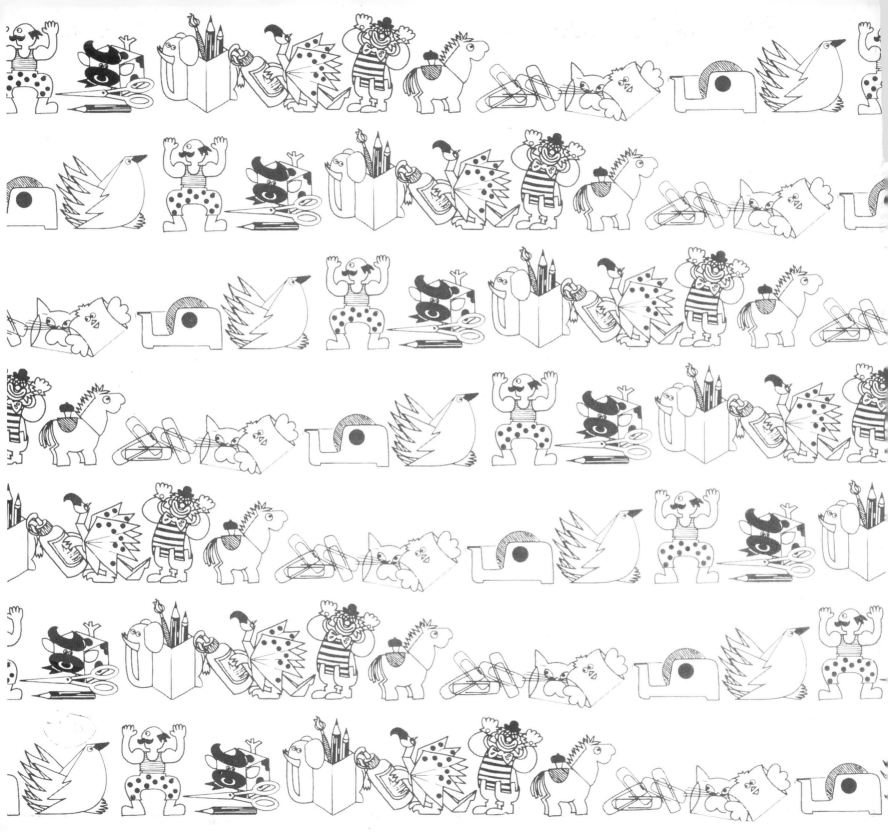